Amidst The Fog

What Silence Left Behind

Nayanthara Ajith

Made with ❤ on the BookLeaf Publishing Platform
www.bookleafpub.in
www.bookleafpub.com

Dedication

To the ghosts of love and the hands that let go...

Preface

These poems were not written all at once- they gathered over time, like mist over still water. Each one is a fragment of clarity found in confusion, a quiet reckoning, a voice that refused to be silenced. *Amidst the Fog* is not about answers, but about standing inside uncertainty and choosing to speak anyway. These verses belong to moments that ached, healed, lingered, and eventually passed; leaving behind a scent, a memory, a poem.

— Nayanthara

Acknowledgements

To those who stood by me when I couldn't see the road ahead: thank you for your quiet strength.

To the ones who left, and to the silences they left behind: you became the ink.

To the readers who find themselves somewhere in these pages: may you feel less alone.

And to the fog itself — for hiding and revealing in equal measure: this book is for you.

1. Smoke-Woven Threads

There was once a window -
opened only once-
where a name clung to rust like scent to old silk.
I hemmed silence into the edge of days,
unfastened the serpent necklace I wore like memory,
and turned from a half-closed door, smiling
as if I hadn't seen it breathing.

I poured tea for a ghost who never asked,
sang to a shadow that never sat.
Some endings don't crash-
they sigh like pages closing, alone.
I reaped the buds of the unsaid truths,
The scent of which belongs never to you,
But to a breeze ever unknown to you..

2. You

You..
The five a.m. teas,
The rise of dawn and the fall of dusk,
Moments slipping quietly between them...
The ocean, the river, and the deep forests-
A pulse, a scent, the taste that lingers on my tongue...
Seasons turning, the moonlight,
Stars that never fade, nights that stretch beyond
measure...
Silence and sound,
The music that flows uninterrupted between...
The truth within,
The letters, the beauty found in emptiness...
The joining and the parting,
The paths that lead me ever back to me...

3. Here I Am, Gone

Here I am, gone -
The words within me, the poems,
buried deep beneath the soil.
At life's midway,
I stand with no one left to claim me.
My heart-
scratched by thorns,
orphaned in its own silence.
This world and I-
belong to me and my despair.
There are no more quests left in me,
no more births waiting to begin.
I...
Here I am, gone..

4. In Your Light

As I walk back
from places where we once met,
memories rise;
soft-footed, tracing
the path we carved in silence.

From the heart of darkness,
lit by the hush of your soul,
I return
to the stillness
where your fingers once shaped
my eyes
with quiet strokes.
There,
the woman within me
gathers herself whole.

And when your tears

fell upon the mark at my temple,
its red dissolved
into a wordless hush—
and you were set free.

5. Whispers of Other Souls

Whose Scars Am I bearing?
Whose wounds am I healing?
Whose sorrows am I erasing?
Whose goodbyes am I wiping away?
Whose stories am I writing?
I... whose soul am I?

Am I the echo of a love forgotten,
the silent plea in the hearts of the lost?
Do I carry the weight of unspoken dreams,
the shadows of lives that never fully bloomed?
In the quiet of my breath,
whose hope do I breathe back to life?
And in the tears I wipe away,
whose brokenness do I carry in my hands?
I...
Whose soul am I?

6. The Last Ember

I burned with him in silent grace,
Now cold and stubbed in that empty place.
He watched me fade once I was gone;
A ghost he sent when love moved on.

Ash clung like memories to the floor,
Flicked away, not wanted anymore.
Smoke curled like the lies we shared,
Dancing slow in stale, spent air.

The fire was brief, the warmth a lie,
He drew me in just to say goodbye.
Now all that's left is a bitter trace;
A warmth once held, now gone without a face...

7. On Silence..

I sparked a flame in a room without windows;
you watched it catch, hands clasped behind your back.
There were stars once, trembling in the dark;
but you called them shadows and turned away.

I stood at the edge where your silence
fell soft and heavy, like snow on a field of glass.
You sketched maps in sand with a borrowed hand,
then cursed the wind for wiping them clean.

I cradled a garden inside my ribs;
you crossed it in boots, crushing the bloom.
A teacup cracked; still warm from the holding.
Your voice clung to the walls
long after your footsteps vanished.

I learned: echo is not a return.
Now, I neither knock nor linger.
The key you once held:
it sleeps in the mouth of the river.

8. In the Quiet of Threads

The narrow footpaths,
Evenings we watched unfold together,
And the blush of my heart you once stirred-
This fading light,
The baby fish in whispering streams,
The paddy fields, the mornings
You rose beside me;
All of it lingers.

This winter's bite,
The merciless heat,
You were my blanket,
My roof above the storms.
The heavy morning fog,
The winding paths through mist,

And the hands that fed me,
The grain you served with tenderness,
Every bite a promise,
Every meal a solace.

Every corner, hums with whispers of you.
You are the thread that wove
The warmth of the world into my skin..

9. Echoes of the Departed

Long for the blue moon,
Be the bare tree beneath its glow,
Walk the moonlit rocks,
For your soul will forever trace its steps alone.
The silence of paths you once chose,
Now crumbles like fallen leaves,
Whispers of promises never kept,
Of roads where shadows never return.
I was but another shadow,
A flicker in your fading light,
As you walked away,
Leaving only the quiet hum of what was never mine to
hold..

10. The Moonflower

When the world folds in on itself,
And the last tree leans into dusk,
When every particle we've ever known
Glows red, then turns to ash;
Melt into me,
Like a moonflower swaying, lost in the dark.
Be the yellow blossoms that bloom only for me.
Let me wear you;
And only you-
Upon my soul.

11. To the Life That Never Took Breath

My crimson heart, veiled in silence...
Behind my clenched and worn-down teeth,
Cries stood frozen, unheard.
Above the waters that refused to flow,
Your fragile life lingered:
Unmelting, unmoving.

A heart that never learned to beat,
Tiny red lips that never knew
The warmth of my breasts.
Somewhere, I heard
The sound of your tears;
Though you were never there to cry them.

From you, I pulled forth
Laughter unborn,
Games never played,
Tears never shed.
Lullabies I sang,

Never meant for the air;
Only for you,
Who never paused to live.

To the life of my life,
Who never found breath to stay...
Without being your mother,
There is no longer a me.
All the love I have left
Was only ever meant for you.
Beyond your memory,
No other soul lives in me.

12. Lunch Box

You were the parcel I unwrapped
without asking why it tasted like home.
The fish-burnt just right,
the kind that stayed on fingers
long after noon.
You were the pickle jars
Wiped against the hem of a sari,
Cups of tea-
Hotter than the boiling noon.
On days the sun refused to forgive,
you were lime water in a cold tall glass..
Fruits you saved without saying,
In a wilted banana leaf,
The broken bit of fish;
You left it untouched; an offering wrapped in quiet.

Let me believe
Those were your ways of loving.

Let me dream,
Just once,
That you drank a cup of tea
Thinking of me.
Let me believe
You saw my smile
In your midday meal;
That I was,
If only in silence,
A part of your plate..

13. Echoes Between Us

You said:
You are mine.
A presence I hadn't known I was missing.
You stayed;
not loudly,
but as if you'd always been there.
There was a stillness in me
that only you understood.
You became the breath between my sentences.
And then
you said:
You have only yourself to return to.
What I choose is mine to carry.
Come no closer;
not every ache is yours to tend.
I never said I couldn't walk away.
So I learned
that love can speak in mirrors,
that warmth and warning
can share the same mouth,

that sometimes
being seen
means being left with nothing
but the echo of being seen..

14. Just Another Sunset

Who knew this light shined on my soul!!
Who knew this train took me to the dark abyss; that's
me!!
Who knew i looked like this through your eyes,
Watching the sun burn into ashes..
Who knew you were holding me tight to let me go;

Who knew the lens you used was borrowed time,
The wind in my hair: a scene you'd framed before;
Me, thinking i was the only sunset you wanted to
remember.
You etched me into golden hour promises,
But handed that same hour to someone else the next
day.

Who knew the warmth i felt was just the fire
Of bridges you'd already lit behind you.
Who knew love could echo,
Even when it was never said with truth.

I was a soft silhouette to you,
But to me, you were the moment i believed in magic.
Now that film plays in reverse,
And i see myself,
Not special,
Just another muse in your gallery of ghosts.

15. Tagged and Traded

You said *I love you*
Before I knew what I felt.
And I mistook it
For something growing...
The first time I let the light touch all of me,
You didn't.
No pause, no wonder;
As if shyness was something you'd seen too often
To name.

You called me "your soul",
Etched it into your skin
Like a vow.
You marked me
In ink and absence,
Called it soul...
But I was only the ending
Of your pattern.

Then left,

Coins folded with goodbye,
A choice dressed as grace.
I stood still,
Your echo inside me,
Turning into something
I never asked to carry.

16. Held and Unheld

Beyond the soul, at time's quiet edge,
By the doors that open, then shut,
I waited, gazing at you...
You wore helplessness like a veil,
Unable to see the love I gave,
Each piece of my heart,
Taken by you,
Unaware.
You turned away,
And whispered, "I will return."
But behind that door, I lingered,
Always, always there..

You, like my father, called me by a name,
A nickname, one only he gave,
And now, you too, spoke it.
You cloaked me in love,
Only to call it something else,
When it no longer suited you.
I did not challenge you-

Fearing the loss that awaited,
I stood behind the door, trembling.

Your hands slipped from mine,
Seeking roots elsewhere,
Leaving me to search for shadows.
With the same small face,
And that same fear of loneliness,
The fear I knew when I was lost in the crowd,
My hands slipping from my father's,
I waited:
My fingers trembling in the silence,

I waited for you,
Beyond the threshold,
Knowing you wouldn't come,
But waiting still...
For you, for us, for our "her",
Our lost love.

17. The Half-Promise

He built a bridge with breadcrumbs;
each one soft with suggestion,
hard with intent.
Not to cross,
but to keep me circling the shore.

He spoke of loyalty
as if it could be halved;
a flame divided
still burning two rooms:
neither of them, mine.

I watched him line his pockets
with secrets stitched
by women who whisper instead of scream.
He called it safety.
I called it silence.

Once, I warned;

don't number me.
Don't fold me into your tale
of wins and wilderness.

But he preferred shadows
over songs,
a life without crescendos,
a ceiling too low for flight.

And I,
who brought candles to his dusk,
learned the art of unburning
myself.

18. Where I Set It Down

There was a weight
that never bruised the skin
but lived beneath every word I didn't say.
I carried it like a secret
folded into the seams of my days,
confusing the ache for love,
and the wait for devotion.

You were a tide I kept returning to,
even as the pull unraveled me.
I gave you not just time;
I gave you the version of me
that still believed love could be enough
if I just stayed a little longer.

But I've learned:
love should not resemble hunger,
should not feel like asking
to be held where you already are.

So I place it here now;
all of it:
the storm,
the quiet,
the poems I never wrote,
the questions I stopped asking.

This is not a plea.
This is not a regret.
This is release.
I loved you bravely.
And I leave you gently.
Not with noise;
but with grace.

19. What the Heart Hoards

I do not gather shame
from the garden where I once poured rain.
You drank freely,
with both hands,
as if thirst had no memory.

You hid me like a prayer
never meant to be answered,
folded behind closed doors,
as if light would betray
what your eyes refused to name.
But I...
I was a flame with no fear of smoke,
a window without curtains,
a name spoken aloud
even in the hush of rooms
that weren't mine to stand in.

You missed me:
The way the wind grieves for leaves

it has already scattered.

But I am not here
to mourn you.
This is my ritual:
not of love,
but of release.

A final laying down
of the ache
I once carried like a thread.
No confessions.
No vengeance.
Just silence,
settling into its rightful place.

20. Letters Never Buried

I pressed words
into the folds of hours
that never arrived.
No ink,
only the hush
between dusk and forgetting.

He didn't return them;
not silence,
not sound.
Just the drift
of something
never quite said,
never quite needed.

I left them
in the curve of unfinished sentences,
where names echo once
and fall back
into the page.

They were not letters,
not really;
only a kind of breath
I mistook for staying.

Now,
they linger,
not waiting,
just weightless-
like dust
that remembers
its first light.

21. Amidst the Fog

Amidst the fog,
I once traced silhouettes
that whispered your name;
half-formed,
half-forgotten,
like the taste of rain on broken stone.

There was a season
I mistook unraveling for devotion;
when even tea steam
felt like forgiveness.
Mornings knew me
as the girl who poured quiet
into cracked cups,
who watched stars
as if they might spell
a different ending.

But love,
even the kind that bruises,

has its flowers.
And I carry them;
gently,
softly,
without letting them turn
to thorns.

Let memory ache.
Let silence stay.
I will no longer reach
for you in the mist,
no longer carve your shape
into every passing grey.

I walk on:
not to forget,
but to remember without burning.
To find warmth,
not in your shadow,
but in the green hush
of spring.
For me.
For the soul that stayed...